Four Sea Shanties
for Flute and Piano
(2013)

Arranged by
Jon Jeffrey Grier

Piano Accompaniment

for Marion

About the Arranger

Jon Jeffrey Grier holds a B.A. from Kalamazoo College, where he studied composition with Lawrence Rackley, an M.M. in Composition from Western Michigan University, studying with Ramon Zupko, and an M.M. in Theory and a D.M.A. in Composition from the University of South Carolina, where he studied with Jerry Curry, Dick Goodwin and Sam Douglas. Jon taught Advanced Placement Music Theory and Music History at the Greenville Fine Arts Center, a magnet school of the arts in Greenville, SC from 1988 to 2019, where he was named Teacher of the Year three times. Awards include grants from ASCAP, the Surdna Foundation, the South Carolina Music Teachers Association, the Metropolitan Arts Council, and the Atlanta Chamber Players. Jon has also been a writer/keyboardist in various jazz & fusion ensembles since 1984. He lives in Greenville with wife Marion and Carolina Dingo Roxanne.

T0020257

Program Notes

A shanty is a work song sung by the crews of merchant sailing vessels beginning in the mid-19th century. Sung without accompaniment, shanties were generally used to coordinate manual labor that involved a large number of sailors working together, such as weighing anchor or setting sail. Shanties have their roots in earlier British maritime work songs and in the work songs of American slaves. Though essentially American and British in origin, the singing of shanties was eventually adopted by the crews of many nations through the era of the great wind-driven packet and clipper ships to the end of the century. With the advent of steam-powered shipping they gradually vanished from shipboard use, as the tasks they accompanied no longer existed. Beginning in the 1920's, sea shanties have enjoyed increasing interest from folklorists and folk musicians.

I. The Flying Cloud

The *Flying Cloud* was a beautiful and enormous clipper ship launched in 1851. In 1853 it set the record for the fastest voyage from New York, around Cape Horn, to San Francisco of 89 days, 8 hours, cutting the average of the day in half. That record stood until 1989. Adding to this remarkable feat was the fact that the navigator was a woman - Eleanor Cressy, the wife of the captain. The ballad about a ship named *Flying Cloud* tells the story of an Irishman who was pressed into sailing on a slaving voyage from Baltimore via Bermuda to West Africa, which led to another voyage as a pirate ship that resulted in the execution of the crew. These events have nothing to do with the actual history of the clipper ship.

The Flying Cloud

My name is Arthur Hollandin, as you may understand
I was born ten miles from Dublin Town, down on the salt-sea strand,
When I was young and' comely, sure, good fortune on me shone,
My parents loved me tenderly for I was their only son.

My father he rose up one day and with him I did go,
He bound me as a butcher's boy to Pearson of Wicklow,
1 wore the bloody apron there for three long years and more,
Till I shipped on board of The Ocean Queen belonging to Tramore.

It was on Bermuda's island that I met with Captain Moore,
The Captain of The Flying Cloud, the pride of Baltimore,
I undertook to ship with him on a slaving voyage to go,
To the burning shores of Africa, where the sugar cane does grow.

It all went well until the day we reached old Africa's shore,
And five hundred of them poor slaves, me boys, from their native land we bore,
Each man was loaded down with chains as we made them walk below,
Just eighteen inches of space was all that each man had to show.

The plague it came and fever too and killed them off like flies,
We dumped their bodies on the deck and hove them overside,
For sure, the dead were the lucky ones for they'd have to weep no more,
Nor drag the chain and feel the lash in slavery for evermore.

But now our money it is all spent, we must go to sea once more,
And all but five remained to listen to the words of Captain Moore,
'There's gold and silver to be had if with me you'll remain,
Let's hoist the pirate flag aloft and sweep the Spanish Main.'

The Flying Cloud was a Yankee ship, five hundred tons or more,
She could outsail any clipper ship hailing out of Baltimore,
With her canvas white as the driven snow and on it there's no specks,
And forty men and fourteen guns she carried below her decks.

We plundered many a gallant ship down on the Spanish Main,
Killed many a man and left his wife and children to remain,
To none we showed no kindness but gave them watery graves ,
For the saying of our captain was: "Dead men tell no tales. "

We ran and fought with many a ship, both frigates and liners too,
Till, at last, a British Man-O-War, The Dunmow, hove in view,
She fired a shot across our bows as we ran before the wind,
And a chainshot cut our mainmast down and we fell far behind.

They beat our crew to quarters as they drew up alongside,
And soon across our quarter-deck there ran a crimson tide,
We fought until they killed our captain and twenty of our men,
Then a bombshell set our ship on fire, we had to surrender then.

It's now to Newgate we have come, bound down with iron chains ,
For the sinking and the plundering of ships on the Spanish Main,
The judge he has condemned us and we are condemned to die.
Young men a warning by me take and shun all piracy.

Farewell to Dublin City. and the girl that I adore,
I'll never kiss your cheek again nor hold your hand no more,
Whiskey and bad company have made a wretch of me,
Young men, a warning by me take and shun all piracy.

II. What Shall We Do With a Drunken Sailor?

The authorship and origin of "*Drunken Sailor*" are unknown; some think it resembles a bagpipe melody. Though commonly thought of as British, the first published description of this shanty is found in an account of an 1839 whaling voyage out of New London, Connecticut, to the Pacific Ocean. It was used as an example of a song that was "performed with very good effect when there is a long line of men hauling together." The tune was noted, along with these lyrics:

Ho! Ho! and up she rises, Ho! Ho! and up she rises, Ho! Ho! and up she rises, Early in the morning.

There is some indication that Drunken Sailor is at least as old as the 1820s.

What Shall We Do With a Drnken Sailor?

Refrain:
Weigh heigh and up she rises
Weigh heigh and up she rises
Weigh heigh and up she rises
Early in the morning.

Traditional verses:
What shall we do with a drunken sailor,
What shall we do with a drunken sailor,
What shall we do with a drunken sailor,
Early in the morning?

Put him in the long boat till he's sober.
Put him in the long-boat and make him bail her.
What shall we do with a drunken soldier?
Put/lock him in the guard room 'til he gets sober.

Put him in the long boat till he's sober.
Put him in the long-boat and make him bail her.
What shall we do with a drunken soldier?
Put/lock him in the guard room 'til he gets sober.
Put him in the scuppers with a hose-pipe on him.
Pull out the plug and wet him all over.
Tie him to the taffrail when she's yardarm under.
Heave him by the leg in a runnin' bowline.
Scrape the hair off his chest with a hoop-iron razor.
Give 'im a dose of salt and water.
Stick on his back a mustard plaster.
Keep him there and make 'im bail 'er.
Give 'im a taste of the bosun's rope-end.
What'll we do with a Limejuice skipper?
Soak him in oil till he sprouts a flipper.
What shall we do with the Queen o' Sheba?

III. Shenandoah

Of unknown origin, this melody likely dates from the early 19th century; it first appeared in print in the July 1882 issue of *Harper's New Monthly Magazine*. It subject is unclear and many sets of lyrics exist. Possibilities include a roving trader's love for the daughter of an Indian chief, a pioneer's (or Confederate soldier's) nostalgia for his native Virginia, or the gratitude of an escaped slave to the river for causing the hounds to lose his scent. *Shenandoah* was sung by the flatboatmen - renowned for their singing - who plied the Missouri and Mississippi Rivers; from there it made its way onto the clipper ships. Of the existing lyrics, these are the most often used today:

Shenandoah

Oh Shenandoah,
I long to hear you,
Away you rolling river.
Oh Shenandoah,
I long to hear you,
Away, I'm bound away,
'cross the wide Missouri.

Oh Shenandoah,
I love your daughter,
Away, you rolling river.
For her I'd cross,
Your roaming waters,
Away, I'm bound away,
'cross the wide Missouri.

'Tis seven years,
since last I've seen you,
And hear your rolling river.
'Tis seven years,
since last I've seen you,
Away, we're bound away,
'cross the wide Missouri.

Oh Shenandoah,
I long to hear you,
And hear your rolling river.
Oh Shenandoah,
I long to hear you,
Away, we're bound away,
'cross the wide Missouri.

IV. Jack Wrack

Jack Wrack (Go to Sea Once More) is a sea shanty about a sailor who once ashore, gets very drunk and loses all his clothing and hard-earned money when a prostitute steals them. Though he has sworn to never work at sea again, this situation forces him to accept a position on a whaling ship bound for the Arctic Sea, having to endure terrible conditions such as the freezing cold. The song urges sailors to avoid strong drink and the hard lifestyle that comes with it. The exact origins of the song can be traced to the English Merchant Navy, likely from the period 1700-1900 (Wikipedia).

Jack Wrack

The first time I went to Frisco, I went upon a spree.
My money at last I spent it fast, got drunk as could be;
I was fully inclined, made up my mind, to go to sea no more!
That night I slept with Angeline, too drunk for to turn in bed.

My clothes were new, and my money was too;
Next morning with them she fled!
And as daily I walked the streets around you'd hear the people roar,
"Oh, there goes Jack Wrack!
Poor sailor lad, he must go to sea once more!"

The first one that I came to was a son-of-gun called Brown.
I asked him for to take me in; he looked on me with a frown.
He says, "Last time you were paid off, with me you chalked no score,

But I'll take your advance and I'll give you a chance
to go to sea once more!'

He shipped me on board of a whaler, bound for the Arctic seas.
The wintry wind from the west-nor'west Jamaica rum would freeze!
With a twenty-foot oar in each man's hand
we pulled the livelong day;
It was then I swore when once on shore I'd go to sea no more!

Come all you young seafaring men that's listening to my song!
I hope in what I've said to you that there is nothing wrong.
Take my advice and don't drink strong drinks,
or go sleeping on the shore,
But get married, my boys, and have all night in,
and go to sea no more!

FOUR SEA SHANTIES
I. The Flying Cloud

Traditional
arranged by Jon Jeffrey Grier

50410009

II. What Shall We Do With a Drunken Sailor?

Flute

FOUR SEA SHANTIES
I. The Flying Cloud

Traditional
arranged by Jon Jeffrey Grier

V.S.

50410009

II. What Shall We Do With a Drunken Sailor?

50410009

III. Shenandoah

IV. Jack Wrack

III. Shenandoah

13

IV. Jack Wrack

50410009

with tap pedalling as needed